AL_
OIKS
NOW

THE UNNOTICED SURRENDER
OF MIDDLE ENGLAND

DIGBY ANDERSON

THE SOCIAL AFFAIRS
UNIT

British Library Cataloguing in Publication Data
A catalogue record of this book is available form
The British Library

ISBN 1-904863-00-0

For Julius, Barbara, John, Frank & Anthony

Printed and bound in the United Kingdom

ALL OIKS NOW

Contents

Glossary   7

1.   Introduction: Giving up, gone away
       and going over   9

2.   In the shopping mall   15

3.   At sport: the swimming pool   25

4.   In the pub   35

5.   At the church   45

6.   On the beach   53

7.   At the airport and abroad   63

8.   At table   71

9.   In court   79

10.   Conclusion: a future for
       Middle England?   87

Biographical note   93

Glossary

Oik *(Chambers Twentieth Century Dictionary)*, a cad, an ignorant, inferior person (colloquial), a chap, bloke (slightly derogatory).
Etymology uncertain.

Oik *(Online Dictionary of Playground Slang)*, a member of the lower classes (UK) especially anyone not English e.g. one who pronounces "i" as "oi".

Oik *(Online Dictionary)*, a person regarded as inferior because ignorant, ill-educated or lower class.

Oik *(Dictionary of Slang)*, oik is hoik, to spit, Bootham School, 1925.

Oik *(Shorter Oxford Dictionary)*, oik (oick), school slang, uncouth or obnoxious person, a fool, an idiot (earlier).

CHAPTER ONE

Introduction

Once upon a time, and for a very long time, Middle England was as solid and immovable as a rock. Shopkeepers easily catered for its enduring tastes and so did the BBC. The Church of England offered it a privileged position and the benches of Magistrates' Courts rung to its moralizing pronouncements. Political pundits keen to predict elections or support for political parties and policies knew it was there and what its habits and prejudices were. It was a minority but a sizeable one and it could be relied on to behave and vote consistently in favour of independence, self-reliance, traditional values especially with regard to the family, and against high taxes, trades unions, foreigners and perverts.

Progressive persons especially intellectuals hated it but the very consistency of its unspeakable beliefs gave them an unchanging enemy to denounce. Denouncing the middle class, even better the lower-middle class or the bourgeoisie, even better the petit-bourgeoisie and best of all the elderly and provincial petit-bourgeoisie never called for much inventiveness since the object of ridicule remained obligingly consistent. A sneer would do. An eminent intellectual once referred to "commuter idiocy". He did not even have to explain. After all, it's common knowledge that commuters are idiots.

I suspect that some of those who used to ridicule Middle England, secretly rather liked it, or, at least, liked its continued obstinate existence. They professionally or personally depended upon it and were emboldened to call for its annihilation safe in the knowledge that it would always be there. Well, it's now gone. It went quite quickly, sometime in the years between 1975 and today. Its absence has not been much noticed. Today, its ancient enemy, the intellectuals continue to rail against it and the complacent majority which has for so long thoughtlessly relied on it to keep society on the straight and narrow, continues to assume it will get them out of trouble. It won't. It has gone. It has surrendered. Yes, there are still people around who think they are Middle England and who may look a little like it. But they no longer have the values and habits that made Middle England what it was. They don't even look very much like it; its devotion to smart, clean but undemonstrative clothes and haircuts is scarcely shared by any income group or age today. So much so that the barbers who used to give manly haircuts in five minutes for £2.50 plus 20p tip and talk about the weather and the cricket have been replaced by perfumed Unisex saloons staffed by ladies who take an hour, charge £12 and talk to each other about the disgusting events of last night's date.

You can use major statistical indicators to show Middle England's decline. In the early seventies ME was, as ever, denouncing lone parenthood and polls found it still implacably opposed to the tolerance of homosexuality. Today, it not only does not denounce lone parenthood, it takes part in it as enthusiastically as the lower classes and when it discovers a homosexual offspring it celebrates the offspring's lifestyle. It once voted for Mrs Thatcher to cut taxes and welfare scrounging. Now it has joined the queue in seeking handouts especially those designed to send everyone, however academically stupid or disinclined, to what passes for a university. By the time poor Mr Major launched his moralizing "Back to Basics", Middle

England had given up basics in its attitude and behaviour and was disenchanted with what had been its most useful function, moralizing. It now rarely talks about right and wrong, it favours prizes for all and talks of "moving forward".

When I say Middle England has gone, I mean that it has surrendered in one or more of three ways. Some Middle Englanders have simply *given up* the values and behaviour that made them what they were. Others weakly hold onto them but are too timid to declare them in public spaces. They have retreated into their homes, *gone away* and left the public stage to the enemy. The enemy, of course, is both the liberal would-be intellectuals and the unrespectable lower orders. This form of retreat can be seen most obviously in supposedly trivial public places, parks, pubs, beaches, shopping malls, churches, trains and restaurants. Some of these ME scarcely enters now, noticeably churches and pubs. Others it goes to but when there looks like and behaves like its old lower class enemies. It even speaks as badly as they do and copies their accents. *Going over – to the enemy* - is the third form of surrender.

It is these public places that this exploratory study is about. I have left the major statistical indicators to others to study. What interests me is to show how the surrender of Middle England can be seen in everyday public places. I want to illustrate it, not prove it. I haven't spent time defining what Middle England is, or, rather, was. But roughly I'm interested in those parts of the upper working, what used to be called the "respectable working class" and middle classes, especially the middle and old aged among them and those living in smallish towns in the provinces. They had various characteristics in addition to those mentioned, some shared with other classes above and below. They exerted strong discipline over their children. They valued orderliness, punctuality, decency, modesty, reticence, amateurishness, deferment of gratification, moderate religion, saving, small shops and speaking properly. They kept themselves and especially their children well away from the (unrespectable) lower classes lest they be contaminated. They were suspicious of people from London. They hated intellectuals and Smart Alecs. They also hated exhibitionism, untidiness and dirt in appearance, public discussion of sex and foreign food. They were proud of their country and its history.

They and their opinions and behaviour have now gone in the sense that they are no longer socially significant. "Good riddance" will be one response. Politicians, consumer analysts and opinion formers can now safely ignore them. The future belongs to those people that the old Middle England called the oiks.

CHAPTER TWO

At the shopping mall

Anyone researching the state of Middle England by direct observation of how its members behave in public places will quickly encounter – and just as quickly overcome – a significant difficulty. How do you tell a Middle Englander? Looking at shoppers for instance, are they Middle-Englanders or members of the unrespectable lower classes, those who used to be referred to as "not our sort of people"? It used to be easy. The MEs dressed differently, held themselves differently, spoke differently. They wore sports jackets or blazers or twin sets or suits and any doubts left by dress were resolved the moment they opened their mouths.

Now Estuary English is BBC English and the middle-aged MEs dress and speak much more like the middle-aged lower orders and both imitate the young of both classes. However they do tend to shop in different shops: the market researchers know where As and Bs and Cs go. And even though the middle-aged MEs try to imitate lower class yobs in their use of certain vogueish expressions, or expressions which were the vogue last year, the imitation is far from a total success. It certainly does not fool the imitated young people.

Why do the MEs want to look and sound like the lower classes and youth? What is significant about it is their *attempt* not the ineffective result. In the past ME devoted considerable effort to maintaining and showing as much difference from the lower classes as possible and in training their offspring in these differences. Their efforts have simply been abandoned or even reversed. They have hauled up the White Flag or even gone over to the other side, the enemy – as was. We shall return to this. For the moment what matters is that the attempt largely fails and so any observer can still tell the MEs from their old enemies in public.

And there is plenty to observe about Middle England in their favourite supermarkets and shops and even in street markets. When I entered the supermarket in the mall, I had a pre-conceived idea that the key issue would be what sorts of products ME bought. That is quite interesting. They buy a lot of food which promises to be "easy" for instance. There is, for example, "easy" garlic, garlic cloves separated, peeled and chopped. Today's shopper must be busy indeed if she cannot afford the 30 seconds required to peel and chop a couple of cloves of garlic.

One can make quite a lot of this easiness business. Old Middle England never sought ease. It revelled in hard, boring work and thought ease corrupting. It would have called it "corner-cutting". It is sometimes said that the modern woman or, occasionally, "new man" is too busy to cook from raw. Processed ready foods may cost more but they enable the family to have two incomes so they are efficient in terms of cost. In fact cooking from raw rarely takes lots of time. What it nearly always demands is discipline and time management. So, for instance the woman-man tasks involved in making bread – mixing, kneading take a couple of minutes. The key is that one must remember to mix the dough so many hours before baking and eating. Similarly, stewing beef cooked in wine may take two minutes to make ready the ingredients but it will need to be cooked anything from four hours to two days before it is needed. What easy foods allow, then, is not so much time as freedom from the need to think and plan about food. They allow indiscipline. ME used to pride itself on its disciplined approach to life. What ME buys today shows off its new values and they are far from the old ones.

But what is even more intriguing than what is bought is the way shopping is done. When MEs go into the supermarket, they take a trolley and they fill it with goods. The operative word is "fill". Most shoppers seem to buy between ten and thirty items. Many of them seem to do a weekly or twice weekly shop. Now, anyone from any social background can remember that she needs lavatory paper and milk, but ten or more items test the memory. ME used to shop with a list, usually secreted in a purse, the purse secreted in a handbag, the handbag secreted in a shopping bag and the list, purse and handbag buried at the bottom of the shopping bag under other bags of purchases already made. This ingenious system meant that the shopping expedition was frequently and suddenly interrupted by halts as the shopper tried to feel down with one hand to find the bag and the purse and extract the list. Lots of little chaoses and spillages and even bumping intos resulted. And great hold-ups occurred when payment had to be made and purses, also deeply buried in layers, were extracted.

It's a long time since I saw a good spillage or hold-up of this sort. And this is not because the shoppers are now all attaching their lists to the little frame thoughtfully provided by the supermarket people on their trolleys. Lists have either gone altogether or shrunk to a shadow of their former glory. Visiting one supermarket, I saw next to no lists being used. But on a subsequent visit I realized I had missed them. Some shoppers do not have lists at all. Those who do, have very small ones. That is how I missed them.

The lists seem to have far fewer items on them than the items in the trolley. And they are on small scraps of paper. The old list on a sheet of lined paper, taken from a stationery pad, carefully prepared and neatly written, reflecting the exact state of the larder and fridge at home, its contents and deficiencies and the anticipated needs of the next few days is gone. It used to group items under headings, The Supermarket, The Dry Cleaners, The Butchers, The Post Office. And as each item was bought and the deficiency made good, it was just as carefully ticked or crossed out. I only saw one person with a pencil crossing out items. The old list-maker might even go further in preparing the list and put affordable costs against each item reflecting an overall weekly budget.

I refuse to believe that either improvements in council schools or in nutrition have propelled such staggering improvements in memory as to make detailed methodical lists redundant. No, the sort of careful shopping that the list helped and stood for has itself diminished. Today the needs of the household are increasingly left to errant memory, chance and, above all, to impulse. The results are surely that essential items are forgotten and unneeded ones bought. But more generally impulse has replaced planning. And you can see it as I did. Just follow Middle Englanders and their trolleys and watch. They do not move purposely to a quarry. They gently slow and stop as something, something they had not planned to buy catches their eye. The same applies to prices. There were few shoppers comparing prices. They seemed to be buying what the shop told them to buy as the "best-buy". The "impulse" did not always come from the trolley-pusher. It might come from accompanying children, "Mummy can we have…?"

Shoppers occasionally pick up items and stare at them. I say "stare" intentionally. They don't seem to be

reading the huge lists of information which, thanks to the demands of unrepresentative food and environmental activists, now litter the surfaces of every packet, tin, plastic container and box. They don't read about sugar levels and impact on dolphins, at least not while shopping. They just stare, look puzzled, purse their lips, put their head on one side, then slip the item into the trolley or put it back on the shelf.

It may be objected that item lists are not essential. There is another sort of list which reads: "Friday breakfast, lunch, dinner, Saturday breakfast lunch, no dinner – going out, Sunday breakfast lunch (remember Dick and Mary are coming to lunch and she doesn't like pork)." This sort of list can be quite short and the shopper only decides on items when she has seen if they look good. However if this list were used, you would be able to see the meals, as it were, in the trolley. There would be the neck of lamb with the leeks and carrots and onions for the lamb stew. In fact, usually the contents of the trolley seem to have no relationship to each other. The majority seem to be items which are not part of composite dishes let alone composite meals. This should come as no surprise because we know family meals are in decline and composed dishes rarely cooked. The modern family eats on the basis of individual impulse. For this sort of eating, impulse and disorganized shopping is, with the aid of a freezer and microwave, perfectly adequate.

The impulse shopping may suit the impulse eating but impulse eating is itself extremely inefficient. And it is very expensive to buy all one's food from one source. Supermarkets are cheaper for many packaged goods such as flour or tins of tomatoes but are much more expensive for vegetable staples such as onions or potatoes. Processed foods are around 50 per cent more expensive than foods cooked from raw. Most costly of all is individualized eating. The effect of four individual members of a family eating separately as and when they feel like it is to inflate costs enormously. The most efficient way to feed four is to feed them together on menus coordinated over three days. The way ME shops is simply improvident and wasteful. Remember what the old ME thought about waste.

The ultimate in wasteful shopping is to be seen in clothes and technology shops but it can also be seen in food supermarkets. It is what is called "Shopping"; by which is meant shopping as an end in itself. People, of all classes, apparently take themselves off to shopping malls and super-markets as they might go to the cinema or beach. They enjoy it in and for itself. There is also, apparently some-thing called "shopping-as-therapy", shopping to help modern Middle England feel good about itself. Super-markets have responded to this new shopping demand and become "outing" places with play areas for the children, restaurants for the adults, benches for the oldies, car clean-ing for the Mondeo and lavatories and ersatz music for all.

And why not? The only point is that Middle England used to cherish as core values, domestic economy, prudence and planning. It only approved of feeling good when it had done good and even then was suspicious about it. It regarded time as something not to be wasted. I saw very little of the old core values in the supermarket. The loss of the detailed list is a sign of a fundamental shift in what Middle England believes in. As a footnote, contrast the new therapy shopping with an activity the old ME used to indulge in which was its exact opposite. It was called window shopping. ME ladies would go to high streets after shops had shut and enjoy themselves looking at the windows of the big stores. Window shopping involved no acquisition and no money was spent.

If impulse has replaced planning, what has replaced budgeting? The answer can be seen at the check-out. As the items roll their way to the check-out girl and are registered and the cost of each displayed, the shopper takes little notice. She is looking around vaguely wondering if she has forgotten something, where her children are or whether the parking meter has run out. I am exaggerating? Well, look what happens when the total arrives and payment has to be made. The old Middle England would have worked out the exact sum due and be ready to forage in the purse in the bag in the trolley for it. Her new Middle England daughter next to never checks the total displayed against some anticipated total and even more rarely challenges it. There has been no anticipated total, indeed no anticipation. As she looks about her, Mrs Middle England holds her right hand just above her waist, the palm upward and the fingers holding her credit card. As the total is declared she moves the hand forward a few inches and proffers the card, often still looking about her. It is taken, swiped and returned with the chit. That is just as quickly and thoughtlessly signed and the transaction is over. There is no need for thought let alone budgeting. Both have been replaced by credit. More, the check-out is now a place which you may leave with more money than you had when you arrived at it. Just mutter "please" to the till-girl's seductive invitation, "cash back?" and, in addition to getting all the goods on tick, you can have a fistful of fivers to blow after you leave.

The new shopping all amounts to lots and lots of credit, an average of £45,000 per family. This mountain of credit, or to give it its old-fashioned name, debt is not restricted to the feckless lower classes. Nearly half of the indebted are homeowners. A study in *The Times* describes typical debtors. A 26 year-old office manager going in for teacher training already owes £10,000 and admits without any recorded shame to "frivolity". Another teacher awaiting training owes £22,000 and is, it seems, happy with it. A report from the Financial Services Authority (both this and the study in *The Times*, 1 August 2003) blames "parents who indulge their children's every whim". They have not been taught to "learn to wait". Patience Wheatcroft on the same page describes a population "no longer prepared to wait for what they want."

Whether such indebtedness is good or bad is not our consideration. What matters for the present argument is that the use and abuse of elastic credit permits impulse buying and makes good, in its own way, lack of planning and excessive expenditure. Even more important the acceptance, even enthusiasm for credit is a complete reversal of Middle England's traditional attitude which was that borrowing is deeply dangerous and owing money dishonourable: "Neither a borrower or a lender be". Even more noteworthy than this, the old ME was obsessed with the virtues of patience, waiting and saving. It was not only prepared to wait for what it wanted, it made a virtue of it, even in some cases enjoyed it. Waiting and saving were part of that discipline that made civilized society and good people, self-control. ME child-rearing was organized around the central concept of learning to "defer gratification". This was what separated them off from the feckless lower classes and criminal classes who could not control their desires.

And what are the children doing while mother is running up the debts with the casual movement of her up-turned hand and her vacant gaze? Not much. Nothing useful, at least. I was watching Middle England shop in the school holidays. So the mothers had their children with them. The children wandered away in the store, came back, asked for things, hung onto the trolley. I saw none being aggressive or naughty. If they caused a nuisance it was because they seemed not to have been taught to look out for other people. They looked at each other, mother, their trolley and some of the goods they fancied. Again, the old ME would have made sure their children "did not get under people's feet". And they would have given them something purposeful to do. Older children might have carried and managed the list. All children would have been used to carrying things. Yet outside the store in the mall and street market, I saw parents struggling with bulging plastic bags. The children, with one exception, carried nothing. ME now not only, as the FSA puts it, "indulges their children's every whim", it requires little ordered effort or activity from them At least in this sort of public behaviour, the canons of child-rearing and good behaviour that defined what it was to be middle class and respectable working class have been abandoned You can look for the old Middle England in a Shopping Mall and it's just not there.

CHAPTER THREE

At sport: the swimming pool

The old Middle England joined rugby, tennis and cricket clubs, went to the swimming pool and engaged in various other sports. It still does. I have chosen to focus on just one of these three and look at behaviour at the swimming pool. Swimmers were always rather dull. Not for them the beer-drinking and bawdy songs of the rugby club. They still are dull but that is not the end of the story.

The swimming pools I visited (which I refer to collectively as "the swimming pool") are found in fitness centres. Outside the building, there is a fair smattering of BMWs and Mercedes. That, and the membership fee of about £1,000 a year says something about the sort of people who use the swimming pool I go to. The fitness centre, besides the pool has courts and a huge torture chamber of weights and exercise machines. You might think the high fees mean the people are middle class. That's broadly true but I think the swimmers are rather different to the weights and exercise people. The swimmers, to be more precise, the swimmers who swim lengths, are also noticeable for their age. There are hardly any children or teenagers. Ages seem to start in the middle to late twenties with a good half post-45. And the pools I visited for this chapter were all in the provinces. This is, then, about Middle England.

We swimmers share a locker and changing room with the masochists from the torture chamber. We swimmers are not masochists: we are, in comparison, persistently and rather admirably, dumb and glum. I have never yet seen an adult swimmer obviously happy. It's not surprising. Swimming up and down is rather repetitive. We swim up to 60 odd lengths. It takes about 25 strokes to do a length. The first stroke is hardly exhilarating but when contrasted with what follows, is an intoxicating experience. The second and third you get used to the sensation, the temperature and surrounding – insofar as chlorine-encrusted goggles allow you to perceive them. Then, after these few seconds comes nearly an hour of the same. The next 1,497 strokes rarely offer any unexpected developments apart from the odd sudden but not exactly threatening wave from a fellow swimmer who is a splasher (crawler). You can gaze at the clock – goggles again permitting – but the hand doesn't seem to move at all, except when you're swimming away from it and thus miss the thrilling, silent, one-minute hand shift. Up to a few years ago, you could count your money and gloat about your investments. Not now. You can try and remember the shopping list.

Just occasionally there's a quarrel: someone gets in a lane and swims more or less speedily than the other occupants. Overtaking results with a consequent irritating wave and about once every six months someone might gently kick someone else. I have never heard harsh words spoken, indeed rarely any words at all. Glum and dumb.

By contrast the sauna is a riot of gossip: "Excuse me, could you turn the sand-timer over? Thanks" and then ten minutes later, "That's me cooked/ That's all I can take/ Phew, I'm off". This banter is not pure self-indulgence. It is really a preparation for the Jacuzzi, a sort of transferable skill. So you just have to say "press" instead of "turn" and "bubble starter knob" instead of "sand timer" and you're a top rank sophisticated conversationalist to match the best of them.

When you arrive in the changing room, be you swimmer or torture masochist, you are greeted by an unpleasant smell. "It was ever thus", I hear you chorus. Yes, but this is not the old smell. That was of leaky pipes, sweat and urine. This is from body sprays. The masochists have huge bags full of nothing much except sprays. They, and it's the men I am talking about (Mrs A tells me the ladies are not like this) take two out at a time (these are young men with muscles, tattoos and stubble), one in each hand, huge long sprays, and spray themselves. Old Middle England, that is, male Old Middle England would not have been seen dead with a perfume spray. If there was one thing it despised, and perhaps feared, it was any sign of effeminacy. Effeminates might turn out to be nancy-boys and even when they weren't they were unmanly, untrustworthy and cowards.

I've never seen swimmers do it. It, spraying, is forbidden by the management for swimmers when in the swimming pool area, but that can't be why they don't do it because swimmers don't look at the notices. Dumb and glum, they are also obviously blind to the helpful warnings and instructions that the management has put up for their education and amusement.

At one count, in one particular swimming pool, there were 192 individual instructions between the entry end of the locker room (near the torture chamber) and the swimming pool. I say at one count because the notices are always being changed or added to. Some, I admit, are repeats but I have not included instances where a whole board of instructions is repeated. Early on one's journey one sees "Girls aged 6 and over are not permitted in the men's changing room", "No liability is accepted for loss of possessions". There are detailed instructions on how to work the nappy bin. Later we are urged to beware of slippery floors and to remove any footwear. The bathing costume drier has its own instructions: make sure nothing (other than your swimming costume) is in the basket and that its waistline strings are pushed down – only one swim suit at a time, etc. This is all repeated a few yards away lest it be missed. There are "Wet area guidelines": these are obviously viewed as especially important because they are repeated several times; always shower and toilet (sic) before using spa, sauna or pool, don't dry any articles of clothing in the sauna and don't take any magazines or newspapers in there. Books are apparently permitted but I have never seen a swimmer with one, apart from me. Just as well, the damp heat destroys the spine and the would-be reader finds himself confettiing the sauna with 300 soggy pages. As far as the swimming pool itself is concerned, barging is out, so are shouting, pushing, smoking, ball games, snorkelling, glass, outdoor shoes and "unseemly behaviour".

Those contemplating the sauna are warned that excess use might make them very hot and of the possibility of dizziness, fainting, burns. If you have high or low blood pressure, kidney disease or indeed any inability to perspire, you should not enter. In the same vein, if you have taken anti-histamines, anti-coagulants, vasco-constrictors or dilators, stimulants, narcotics, tranquillizers, a meal or alcohol within the last hour and a half, beware the sauna. Whole groups are not allowed to use the sauna, the young and the old, the pregnant and people wearing jewellery.

As I say, I've never seen a swimmer reading these. This is not surprising because most of the notices are misplaced and mistimed. It's not much fun for a snorkelling-mad pregnant lady whose just had a three course lunch and a bottle of Chardonnay to set aside an

afternoon, organize a taxi, get down to the fitness centre, change, shower and "toilet" and only then, at the last minute be confronted with notices telling her she can't swim, sauna or do anything else. Most people have seen brochures when they joined and been told of the rules by someone else so that the display of the instructions is pointless. Or rather it is pointless for the swimmers. It is not pointless for the management. It points to the extent to which England has become a liability and victim culture.

Many of the instructions are commonsense. When the swimmers appear to be obeying them, they are really just being sensible. When the instructions are silly, the swimmers ignore them. So someone having a swim, then a sauna and steam room may have four showers but is not likely to attempt four "toilets".

And in another way, the swimmers' behaviour is rather impressive. There is a tradition in England of amateurism. One part of it is a disdain for exhibitionism, flamboyant effort and equipment. The English golfer or shooter used to wear a simple country suit, perhaps plus fours and was proud to use his father's old clubs or gun. On the golf course, at least, this tradition is nearly dead: showy vulgarity reigns. But the swimmers in general maintain it. True there is the odd chap who will arrive with a bag of toys, things to shove between his legs so he can practice swimming arms only or nasty plastic caps. Such exceptions will also sometimes ostentatiously fiddle with their goggles at the end of the lane or pointedly examine their watches. One in a hundred swimmers will dive demonstratively into the pool shouting "Oh": diving is one of the dozens of things forbidden by the notices.

But most swimmers arrive silently, clad in black or blue, dull costumes clutching neatly rolled plain towels, most of the ladies in one-pieces not bikinis let alone "thongs". They go straight to the edge, slip into the water, swim up and down and get out and leave as quietly as they came. They seem to show that England today can still boast a culture which values self-improvement, orderliness, commonsense and quiet worthiness. Dull but decent; that's the swimmers. Or are they? Unfortunately this happy picture is an illusion, or, more accurately, a remission from the normal state of affairs. You see these are not the only swimmers. Other swimmers include several types who exhibit none of the dull virtues of Middle England. There are the torture chamber people who decide to have a swim after their weights or machine walking or stretching. These are not proper swimmers at all. The men among them splash and shout and the women try to swim in pairs talking about their hairdressers and disturbing the proper swimmers' lanes as they try to keep abreast. Occasionally the ladies arrive en masse for something called aquasize. They commandeer half the pool. Their instructress switches on loud music and then has to shout at the ladies over the music instructing them to jump up and down in the water. The ladies are fat, and forty of them jumping up and down make waves for the poor swimmers to swallow. The din is frightful.

Then, among the not-proper-swimmers I should also mention those learning to swim in formal lessons. They, mostly young children, are far less of a nuisance than the fat jumping ladies. What is bizarre about the lessons is how long they go on for. I can recall, from my childhood, two distinct methods of teaching children to swim. One was to give them a rubber ring to swim in and then at some point they would discard it and swim. Another was to show them doggy paddle and throw them in. Now there are whole "terms" in which the children and their Mummies play about in the water to nursery rhymes "building confidence in the water" with "buoyancy aids", more terms in which the "teacher" introduces the children to the "lesson environment with and without aids", then on through different strokes and distances, years and years of it. Old Middle England would have scorned all this as "making an unnecessary fuss or show about it".

Then again, there are those who one might call improper swimmers. I suspect they are adulterers: middle-aged couples who arrive separately and stand at one end of a lane ogling and sometimes kissing each other and blocking the lane for proper swimmers. It may be, of course, that they are happily married – to each other. But that makes their behaviour even worse. What is, or would have been totally unacceptable to respectable England is the public display of affection especially any form of touching. I admit that there are not many adulterers in the pool. That is not the point. The point is that the rest of the swimmers show no signs of being shocked by this behaviour. And that is a great change.

However the most important evidence that one should not trust the favourable impression of contemporary Middle England created by the morning length-swimmers is what happens in the afternoon. Apart from brief visits from the torture chambers persons, adulterers and learners, the morning scene is of quiet dull swimmers ploughing up and down in their lanes, not saunaing for an hour and a half after their wholemeal sandwiches and showering, if not toiletting, time and time again. Around 3.00pm the first mother and child, less frequently, Daddy and child appear. Within half an hour the pool is full of children shouting squealing, swimming across lanes, barging, running round the "wet area", not showering and not toiletting, at least not in the toilets and engaging in all manner of "unseemly behaviour". No doubt if they could, they would go in the sauna with kidney problems or full of cocaine. Adult swimmers retreat to the sauna and watch the chaos through the steamy glass. And they all say the same thing: "Ghastly kids, but it's not their fault, you know. Why won't their parents control them?"

What is remarkable is the contrast between the behaviour of the dull, decent adults with their own age group and that of the parents and children. For many of the parents who are so irresponsible when with their children are the same people who are so good and dull when swimming on their own. And what goes for the swimming pool goes for the park and the train and the street.

It is true that more spectacular betrayals of the old code of Middle England can be found elsewhere. You will find the new Middle England shouting at cricket matches, for instance. Shouting is also a form of exhibitionism, one to be seen at many sporting events today, even those such as cricket which used not to have it. The old ME used to watch cricket. That is, they sat and watched it. The game, the players were the spectacle and the spectators were, well, spectators, watchers. Increasingly the spectators are the watched. They are attracting attention themselves. They shout. They stand up and down in synchronized attention-seeking surges. And the crowd's behaviour has become a topic of media interest in its own right.

The spectators used to applaud good play by their own side and by the opponents and deplore bad play regardless of who was responsible. Modern spectators cheer on their own side regardless. The crowd used to help sustain the moral order of the game. Now like the players they subvert it. And they look the part, scruffy and noisy and frequently drunk. Games, especially cricket were a way in which various virtues, some of them aristocratic in origin, were inculcated in the middle classes at grammar and public schools. Fair-play, courage, recognition of the opponents' dexterity or courage, submerging one's own opportunities and fame in team work and an English self-deprecation were part of the morality of the better games. Now with the cult of the celebrity and the crowd, the rise of win-at-any-price including cheating and the dismissal of amateurism, games have ceased to be a place for the old Middle England.

All these breaches of the code of old Middle England are by definition more spectacular than what happens at the swimming pool with children. Yet it may be that the failure to control children at the pool and in other public places is of even more social significance.

CHAPTER FOUR

In the Pub

The behaviour of Middle England in the pub tells us not so much what the new Middle England is like but how it has retreated from a public space it once occupied. I suppose this retreat from the pub, and indeed other public spaces could be seen as cowardice or lack of self-confidence. Middle England no longer feels itself to be mainstream English culture. It is in retreat.

At the Mucky Duck (White Swan), most Friday evenings today are busy, the busiest evening of the week. Among the mainly Middle-England customers in the village pub are six or so who are of particular interest. Some are in middle age, some retired. They are the last of a dying type. The clues as to the type are their loud enthusiasm for beer, though they do not drink as much as they did, their conversation about sport especially rugby and their loud bonhomie especially their calling each other by nicknames ending in "ers" and a love of banter and stories about escapades. They are the last of the Hearties. I knew Hearties when they really flourished in the Fifties and early Sixties. Hearties came from middle class families. There was perhaps a tendency for their fathers to be farmers or military men but they could equally well be in the professions or business. Hearties were members of rugby clubs and liked drinking beer, the tankards cradled against the chest in the right hand, the left pushed down their substantial bottoms on the inside of their trousers, driving sports cars and playing unintellectual pranks. They liked singing mildly rude songs with easy-to-remember choruses, they liked (partly for the same reason) "traditional" jazz and lurching about ineptly on dance floors with girls called Fiona whom they had met at Young Conservative hops. They sported cravats, cavalry twill trousers, suede Chukka boots and sports jackets. They despised oiks – the lower classes – and foreigners and hated intellectuals, the arts, effeminate persons and anyone who didn't see the obvious merits of rugby football. Although they could be noisy and tipsy, they were far from being deviants. Indeed they were stalwart Middle Englanders just enjoying themselves a bit before becoming estate agents or whatever. Even in their prankish years they spoke properly, were Conservative, conservative, patriotic and respectable.

Various social types come and go, especially those attractive to youth such as Teddy Boys or Hippies. Hearties were different. When a Hearty reached early twenties, got married and started estate agenting or farming, he did not stop being a Hearty. Precisely because Heartiness was not essentially deviant, he could carry on, if confining the beer to one night a week now. Traces of the dress lingered and so did traces of the banter. Unlike so many other types, Hearties lasted. Evelyn Waugh describes them at Oxford in the 1920s having wars with Arties and they were still an easily discernible type at universities and still having wars with the Arties right up into the Sixties, maybe beyond. But now there are no more new recruits, just a few, ageing Hearties on Friday nights. And even then they are failing. Hearties are not safe. Friday night is popular with other people too: the pub is increasingly invaded by young trendies drinking silly drinks out of pink bottles. By 7.30, the old Hearties have had enough: they retreat back home to safety.

The point of interest is that the Hearties were one part of Middle England that colonized pubs. And when

Hearties were in a pub, they took over at least their part of it. Both in reality and fiction, as Hearties and in other types, Middle England held sway in not a few pubs. Bulldog Drummond was a pub man. So was the young Evelyn Waugh. Many middle-class students, those not attracted by other students in the "Union" bars, went to pubs. The doctors of "Doctor in the House" fame liked pubs. Chaps from the City had a couple in the pub before catching the train home. The point is a simple one: the pub was part of – some – middle class lives. Put it round the other way, a visitor, say, an American, when he went into a "typical" English pub would not necessarily be seeing working-class life. He might well especially in the south of England and in villages, be seeing middle class life. To be tediously sociological, the accents he heard, the interests and attitudes he heard expressed in them, the manners he might see might well be middle class. The landlord himself might well be middle class. One stereotypical landlord was the retired wing-commander or naval captain.

A few pubs were exclusively middle class. In others, different social classes and sexes used the different private, jug, saloon/lounge and public bars; the last two differentiated by carpet and price. In many more space within a bar was delimited by class or sex, for instance the ladies sitting at tables by the walls and the men at the bar, a knot of businessmen standing by the fire, some young people in a sort of alcove playing darts. In yet others, there was a shift system. My father always taught me that "they" went home immediately after "their" factory work, had tea and emerged at 8pm to drink. "We" drank from six, "when the ashtrays are clean and the landlord sober" and returned home to dinner at eight. This had the advantage for us, that "we" missed meeting "them", and no doubt for them that they missed meeting us.

I don't want to overdo it. No doubt over the whole of the United Kingdom there were more working-class pubs and working-class people in pubs than there were middle-class pubs and middle-class people in them. That is hardly surprising since there are, or were, many more of "them" anyway. But the middle class had a place in pub life.

Pubs have changed a lot and various interest groups applaud or bemoan the changes. There's more lager, less beer, proportionately more women, fewer men, more young, fewer middle-aged people, more food, less darts and cribbage, more canned music, less singing, more standardisation, themes and reliability, less individual character and seriously "off" beer. Lefty interest groups blame the "big brewers" for the changes they deplore. I am more interested in what has happened to the middle classes and pubs.

Pubs are about sociability, being ready to talk with others. Sociability does not necessarily mean loquacity, being talkative, talking a lot or with a lot of people. It might just be a first customer muttering about the weather or the news with the landlord as the first pint was poured. Sometimes groups that talk together come into the pub already formed, for instance three businessmen from the same company or a group of students. Sometimes exchanges start up in the pub between strangers or people who only know each other in the pub. Conversations start and stop, groups of talkers come together and disintegrate. Most without obligation. This is fairly neutral ground.

Put the points about sociability and the middle class together. They mean that once there was a form of middle-class sociability in English pubs. It is only right to add that this sociability was also largely male and to an extent adult. Of course there were pubs, bars and spaces in bars for the young, but the pub was generally not a

youthful institution. Today male, middle-class, middle-aged sociability in pubs is increasingly rare. Has it been pushed out by the brewers anxious to attract the young and female custom? Or have youth and the lower class and women themselves edged it out and taken over? Or has it committed some form of cultural suicide itself?

Some examples. The Red Lion is a fairly ordinary building about 100 years old situated in a provincial town just within commuting distance of London. It had a saloon bar and a public bar. Every evening between 6 and 8pm, the saloon bar was the meeting place for half to a dozen local shopkeepers, professional people, the odd London commuter just returned home. They drank well, a few pints but mostly large Scotches or gins and tonics. They paid their way. They also talked well about cricket, stories in the news, politics only insofar as it affected them which they considered to be in the form of taxes or unpunished criminals, about their holidays, each other and their families. A small minority of the conversation was taken up with predictable opinions which were aired neither aggressively nor in embarrassment about criminals, foreigners, scroungers, young people and the other social classes. The relaxed way they spoke, leaning against the bar proclaimed their right to be there with their interests and opinions. For about an hour and a half that space was their club.

In the late Sixties, one landlord put in more tables and started cooking and serving food. That brought in a new customer, people who only came at most once a week. The food smelt, a waiter bustled about, it took longer to get drinks, it was noisier. But it did not affect the club. It continued, its members their backs turned to the diners carried on as before. I seem to remember that at some later point anodyne musack was introduced and fizzy beer and raffle tickets and a kitchen and dining extension. But the club kept going regardless. Only death depleted it. Even its effects were limited as, up to the Sixties, several of the members' sons, took their fathers' places.

Twenty five years later, the landlord retired. Another arrived. This time things turned out very differently. Times had changed. He gutted the place, restyled it and, most significant of all, filled it with customers from his own previous pub who talked about football, sex and the price of second-hand motor cars. The old regulars left, the club folded. Could the club have resisted and maintained its place? Perhaps. What destroyed it was partly that it no longer had the favour of the landlord and was outnumbered by the new contingent which had. Yet even this would not have mattered if it had not been depleted. And its depletion was not the fault of the new landlord or the restyling. It was simply that several offspring of the old club members no longer kept up the pub tradition.

Instead they chose, or their wives chose for them, to stay at home. The few who wished to keep going to a pub went to different ones which made them even more outnumbered and beleaguered. One or two of them even reinvented themselves, went over to the enemy and acquired a loquacious interest in football, sex and used cars. The point is that the Middle England presence was not ousted by the landlord or the brewer but by itself, by a new tendency to withdraw into the home.

What happened with The Coach and Horses was similar. For some 30 or more years a Middle England club kept going. Members died or were taken into nursing homes, yet somehow they were replaced by others and not necessarily from their families. This particular club specialized in stereotypical WWII Wing-Commanders and Indian Army Colonels with appropriate moustaches and banter. As one Wing-Commander or Colonel faded from the scene, somehow, defying the passage of time and forces of nature, another would arrive and slip onto the still warm barstool. There was a barmaid, herself in her sixties. The Colonels winked at her and she served them ahead of strangers who had been waiting longer.

The bar eventually closed. Again depleted, the few remaining members somehow did not have the oomph to get together and go somewhere else but went their different ways, which for some meant home. I would not want to say that it is all a matter of retreat by the members. The activities of the pub owners and landlords and managers play some part. It's a vicious circle but one initiated by the members. Their lack of persistence, their cultural weakness reduces their numbers and when opposing cultural forces introduce musack, vulgarity, lefty opinions, bad language and aftershave, the members feel still weaker and retreat again. The retreat ends at home, in front of the television, with a gin and tonic whose measures are monitored by the wife.

The third and last example merely shows another sort of retreat. In this case a pub where the Middle England club met six nights a week had a change of landlord. For a variety of reasons he did not appreciate the members. So most of them reduced their visits to once a week. The pub is entirely different on that night from all the others. A few of the members, as with the first pub, showed yet another response. They stayed and became like the young and lower-class people who replaced the club. Rather as with the pigs in Animal Farm, they even look like their old enemies.

There are then, three ways in which Middle England responds to rival and enemy cultural forces in the pub. Some abandon their positions and flee into the safety of the home. This is especially tempting given the "home" as a source of Middle England pride and identity. Their desertion leaves their colleagues even more outnumbered and threatened by ever more unpleasant developments from their enemies at the pub, such as karaoke. Most of the colleagues then go their own ways to other pubs where they are isolated. A despicable few buy earrings and running shoes, learn dirty jokes, drink American beer from bottles and go over to the enemy. In all three cases, the club and the class has not stood its ground.

CHAPTER FIVE

At the church

As late as the nineteen nineties, John Major drew on the image of a respectable lady cycling home from the eight o'clock Communion service. He had, rather typically missed the boat – but only just. For most of the twentieth century the C of E was widely seen as a church of the middle class, the middle aged or elderly and of market towns and villages in the provinces. And this has a factual basis. None of the churches in England had much success with the unskilled lower classes. Roman Catholicism was a partial exception with the Irish in England and later in the twentieth century so was Pentecostalism. But the appeal of the Non-Conformist churches at least in England was largely to the lower-middle class and respectable working class.

The C of E was the Established Church and also the church of the established values. If ever there was a sphere in life in which Middle-England values held sway it was in the C of E and geographically in the local parish church. There, until the 1970s you could hear the voice of moderate middle-class values in Received Pronunciation perhaps a retired major and a local solicitor as sidesmen and the GP's wife reading the lesson. The vicar, even by then, rarely conformed to the fool of the family type popularized by Kind Hearts and Coronets or the stuttering, asexual twit image but his wife might still be giving violin lessons or supply teaching. And in politics the C of E was known and derided as the Conservative Party at prayer long after its clergy, at any rate, had defected to the Liberal Party.

In fact, for the last forty years of the twentieth century the leadership of the C of E had been far from Conservative politically. It espoused a variety of sentimental uncosted socialism, as famously shown in the denunciation by the Bishop of Liverpool and others of Thatcherism, the demands for ever more public expenditure in Faith in the City and more recently in the idolatrous worship of the United Nations and unrestricted human rights to everything. A survey carried out in the 1980s of C of E pronouncements on social and political issues found next to no conservatism, let alone Conservatism and a good deal of hand-wringing liberalism.

The C of E's leadership has also been liberal in its policies on moral, theological and liturgical matters. It has soft-pedalled on abortion, colluded in new tolerance of single parenthood and divorce and would like to have colluded in the affirmation of active homosexuality. It has embraced a secular agenda on "minority" rights and the role of women and conducted a war against traditionalism in all forms especially in the language and music of church services. This has been done on the liberal grounds of fashionable "inclusivity" and also of a more long-standing but equally vacuous attempt to be "relevant" to young people.

There is a view, for which I have some sympathy, that this liberal agenda was foisted on the Church by its leadership. Certainly some explanation is needed to show why the Church of Middle England should have become a champion of all that Middle England does, or, rather did abominate. The new structures of synodical government provided fertile ground for activists. Their activism combined with a rather new sort of bishop whose background was not so much the parish as quasi-intellectual work in a theological college made the leadership increasingly unrepresentative.

In a sense intellectuals whether in or out of the church are part of the middle class though they hate it and it has traditionally hated them. The middle class has long spawned offspring whose mission becomes to devour or at least sneer at its parents. There is no surprise in that. What is odd, and much more interesting for this study is the way that the Middle England membership of the C of E has gone along with the liberalisation initiated by the elite and activists.

But just before we look at the pathetic spinelessness of the Middle Englanders, the central fact about the C of E should be mentioned, its decline. The church has lost more than half its membership. Congregations are down, baptisms and confirmations (ie, new entrants) catastrophically down, rites of passage (marriages and funerals) down, income down, capital down and bankruptcy looming, and positive influence on national life at an all-time low. This chapter is not, however, about the state of the Church but the state of Middle England. And what the decline means is that, since the Church was largely a Middle-England phenomenon, Middle England has changed. Bluntly, Middle England is far less C of E or even Christian than it was. In a sense ME has changed, in this respect, more than the lower classes which were never much in the Church at all.

So when you go into an aggregate sort of church I shall call St Peter's the first thing you notice is that it is three-quarters empty. ME has forsaken it. The rump that remains has largely if unenthusiastically gone along with the liberal elite's many unsuccessful wheezes for re-filling the churches. Consider some of the things they now do and don't do in St Peter's. As you pass through its porch you see a notice. It is a big notice and obviously thought to be important by the parish priest who has put it up. It is not home-made but bought. It is produced then in some numbers and the problem it is meant to deal with is obviously widespread enough to justify mass production. It reads "Silence" in big letters and asks the congregation if they would please "talk to God", that is say their prayers, before the service and then, after the service "talk to each other". And sure enough as you enter the church you are greeted by the hum of the rump congregation totally ignoring the notice and nattering away to each other, their gossip punctuated by the odd mobile phone going off. This church may have the Blessed Sacrament reserved, that is, God may be really present there. It may not, but even then, it is still the house of God, a place demanding awe, humility, trepidation. The old ME never chattered like this. If they talked at all it was in a whisper. Nattering is not only bad for reasons to do with religion, it is impolite. And look at the natterers. Once they came in their "Sunday best". Now even the servers who assist the priest in cassocks, have their filthy trainers and red socks sticking out from underneath.

The service starts with a hymn, perhaps with choruses displayed on an overhead projector. Well it isn't really a hymn. It's a song accompanied by a guitar. The accompaniment is what you might have expected to find in a second-rate pop song of thirty years ago. So is the predictable syncopation and so is the nauseating sentimentality of the words, all about being nice and treating God's world, our environment, nicely. If there is one thing old Middle England disliked more than scruffiness and impoliteness, it was sentimentality. Yet that is the central characteristic of the entire service.

In fact, there was something old Middle England disapproved of more than scruffiness, impoliteness and

sentimentality, it was "not speaking properly". Old ME rehearsed its children in speaking properly. It kept them away from oiks so they wouldn't catch bad habits and wind up speaking badly. Far-from-rich ME families even sent children to elocution classes. Speaking properly was partly a matter of accent and non-received pronunciation was not approved of. But it was also a matter of not speaking lazily, of not whining and slurring, of speaking grammatically. Since St Peter's has succumbed to the liberal diktat of "participation" and the promotion of minorities, its lessons, intercessions and notices are all read by lay people chosen for their social characteristics (young, black female, disabled) rather than any ability to speak. And of course they can't speak properly, indeed some churches prefer that they do not speak properly. The same sort of social liberalism is shown on the church's walls which are covered not with reproduction religious paintings by artists who painted well but by splodges crayoned by children.

The layman reading the intercessions has been chosen for his uncanny ability to put stress wherever it should not fall and to grunt. Not only does he speak badly: he has been encouraged to invent his own intercessions and no-one has told him how to do it. So he takes everyone on a global tour of wars and famines with no evident thought as to why Liberia, say, is mentioned and Malawi, say, is not. It is accompanied by a little America and global-capitalism bashing but even that is not thought out. It is careless, second-rate tosh. The parish priest is little better. He is one of those people who pick up fashionable phrases just after they become fashionable and fail to weed them out when they fall out of fashion. He twice calls the congregation "you guys" and is careful to say "cool" prefaced by a short pause so it should be noticed just before using it to describe one of Our, and one must charitably imagine, his Lord's miracles. He also says "absolutely", "caring" and "supportive" and urges us all to "relax" in our Christian lives.

The high spot of the service is something which would have made any old Middle Englander flee in embarrassment. It is a variant on sentimentality but it is doubly, or would have been doubly offensive because it also involved physical contact with persons not in one's family, and this contact made in public. The congregation is invited to show each other the sign of peace. Whereupon supposedly respectable elderly people, the sort of people who would not have said more than "Good-morning" to a new neighbour for six months, hurl themselves into the arms of as many strangers as possible during the allotted time of three minutes. Jaws sag and breath is expired as they intone, "Peeeeace be with you", or, in the case of the Intercessor, "Peace, Er, be, Er, wiv yer."

I was once asked to advise a rather senior journalist about this. He had just started attending his local church after moving house into a new district. He found this display of fake emotion rather unpleasant and wanted to know how to avoid it. I suggested that just before the hugging was due to start, he should fall on his knees and bury his head in his hands in prayer. They would, in my experience then pass him by and go and bother someone else. I had not reckoned with the total disregard for other people's feelings and intolerance of traditional habits which now characterizes the worst of Middle England. Poor C was hauled to his feet and forced to be hugged.

Perhaps he should have tried, "No thank you I'm English, we don't do that" or just "B* off". The hugging peace-niks are not the only ones who should be told to b* off. The modern church has deliberately set about recruiting and training a special group of people to drive newcomers out of church and make sure they never come back. Many of the good church people I know are returnees. They left the church in their teens and returned to it at some age between 20 and 60. What made the return, the first time back at church, easy for them, they say is that they could quietly slip into church and leave without questions, without commitments, without having to participate. In many churches such a person would now be met by one of a team of greeters who would invite him for coffee, ask his name, tell him her name, introduce him to the parish priest and shake his hand, in short drive him away. Don't these people know that in the old Middle England neighbours don't say "hello" until they have been neighbours for six months?

There are, to be sure, priests and congregations who have fought off the wheezes of the liberal leadership of the Church. There are others who have been forced to accept them by threat of closure, non-replacement of priest or other pressures. But if we are interested in the way Middle England itself has changed, then a third group is most significant. They have followed the leadership. In so doing, some commentators might suggest they have abandoned their religion even more surely than those MEers who no longer go to church. But more to our point, they have abandoned the attitudes, values and behaviour of Middle England.

CHAPTER SIX

On the beach

Actually, in the town I'm thinking of, they call the beach "the sands". Only visitors call it "the beach". The visitors also often refer to the harbour as "the pier" when they mean "the jetty". The jetty is at one end of the sands which stretch about a third of a mile and curves round to protect them. That and various other natural features such as on-shore winds, which are too boring to discuss mean that the sands are a safe place for children. When I grew up in the town, I and most children were left free to wander about the sands, unsupervised, to amuse ourselves on the rocks, the paddling pools, making putty with the chalk from the cliffs, running up and down the water's edge trying to shush a spray of sea water up the skirts of "old" ladies who were watching over their grandchildren in the sea.

Surprisingly, in this age so obsessed with safety, there are still children to be seen there left to their own devices. Occasionally one gets lost, finds its way to some form of adult authority such as the Red Cross hut and a nasal announcement is made across the Orwellian system of loudspeakers, "Nnnnlist childe, nnnlist childe, leetle girl, answers to the name Chlorine, would parents please collect from the Red NNNCross hut by the main steps?"

In my day there was no Orwell system and I never knew anyone called Chlorine - at least that is what it sounds like, it's something "ine" and not Pauline. Lost girls then were always Mary, Anne or Elizabeth. Boys did not get lost. The worst that happened to boys was that they buried each other in the sands and occasionally, well, once in my childhood, one suffocated and died; at least that was the rumour with which parents tried to frighten little boys from burying each other. It did not work. In August, boys ate wasps and were duly stung on the tongue. The wasp was popped into the mouth clinging to a jam sandwich or doughnut, or buried in an extremely sticky candyfloss. There's not much candyfloss about now. It is replaced by warm soggy chips with tomato ketchup, taken five times a day. The ketchup is sweet enough but the wasps don't seem to like it so there are fewer shrieks and swollen tongues on today's beach.

Still it's rather encouraging just how much is the same. And not only in the way children are unsupervised. I said there were sorts of adult authority figures on the sands but they were and are of the weakest sort. I have never, not once in fifty plus years, seen a policeman on the sands. The nearest to authority are the deck-chair hire lady, the Red Cross, or St John's Ambulance volunteers, the people who run the Punch and Judy show and the man who hires out kayaks. Not exactly Leviathan at his most terrifying.

There are persons who fancy they have authority. These are the lifeguards. There used to be just one and he used to be called the safety-boatman. When the sea was calm, he dozed in a rowing boat anchored in the bay. We used to swim out underneath the boat and bang on its bottom. When the sea was rough, he would land, hoist a red "Dangerous to Bathe" flag and retire to the pub. We carried on swimming of course. I don't recall anyone ever drowning. The safety-boatman was old, at least he appeared old to children. He has now been replaced by a team of young persons with dyed hair, earrings and shorts who speed about in noisy smelly boats and order swimmers to stop doing whatever they are enjoying doing. But no-one takes any notice of them. And mentioning notices, that is one difference between the sands of yesterday and today. Then, the "Dangerous to Bathe" flag apart, there were no notices. Now there are notices about the level of water purity, directional signs to the lavatories, lists of dates when dogs may be taken on the beach, colour-codings of a variety of bathing flags, orders about litter, some of these emanating from local political-bureaucratic busybodies, some from Westminster and even some from Brussels.

But no-one takes much notice of the notices. Or if they appear to do so it is for other reasons. There are few dogs on the sands in the summer not because Brussels has banned them but because there never were. Dogs don't like sitting for hours in the hot sun and their owners know this. Sometimes the orders are simply and ostentatiously disobeyed. Thus, the authorities have designated one part of the sands for swimming and another for the launching of boats. No-one sitting on the sands in the boat launching area wants to walk all the way along to the other area to bathe so they swim where forbidden. This has the additional advantage that it is not patrolled by the bleached-haired safety youths because no-one is expected to swim there.

There are, of course, too many notices and restrictions. But not as many as one might expect. There are aspects of beach life which appear totally unregulated, and the most obvious is the donkeys. There are now two donkeys. There used to be six. They give shorter rides now and no longer display their names on their foreheads. Otherwise they are the same. One thought about the donkeys: these donkeys carry small children. The small children might fall off and hit their heads on one of the flint stones that lurk in these particular sands. Should not the children wear safety-helmets and be strapped on securely with safety belts? Should not the donkey owners be forced to display safety advice and disclaimer forms in eight languages? Are the donkey operatives trained? Should not the donkeys themselves wear sun visors? Why are their faeces not examined for dangers to beach contamination? Enough, but you see the point: the donkeys, the little fun-fair at the other end of the beach, the candyfloss, are a bureaucrat's potential Utopia. Yet nothing has been done. Somehow the sands escape the modern obsessions of the rest of society

The most extraordinary thing about the sands was that there was never any trouble. In the old days there might be over a thousand people on the sands and they would be forced to be quite close to each other. Yet I never heard any harsh words let alone saw physical conflict. It is extraordinary; you would think all those people, out in the heat. It's not that they didn't do anything that might have upset each other. They shook their towels and the sand blew in their neighbours' faces or onto their candyfloss. The children shouted and ran and accidentally kicked sand over the oiled bodies of tanning ladies, children and sometimes adults threw water at each other, missed and hit bystanders and even worse bysleepers. Balls, Yo-Yos and shuttlecocks hit old ladies. But no-one reacted with anything more than a "Tut".

And that, in crime-ridden England is still true. On this beach at any rate, people get along pretty peaceably. I have three explanations. First, the town is middle class and the beach is known as a family beach. Elsewhere there are beaches fit for surfers or ones with mass entertainment. Second, and relatedly, both then and now, teenagers, the source of so much crime, trouble, noise, rudeness and unloveliness in the wider society, were and are under-represented on the sands. Something happens to boys and girls at about thirteen. They see the beach as a place for

children and oldies. They can't show off their equipment, whatever is the latest prized possession on the beach or indeed the latest clothes. Being nearly naked means that standing out and cutting a fine, fashionable figure is difficult. Even the latest hairstyle when a north-east wind has done its worst and the hair is thick with sand, looks much like anyone else's. Every now and then you see a teenager trying to show off a fetishistic possession. Along the beach he comes trying to wheel his new bicycle. It may have just the latest style of handlebars and wheels and seat but the wheels get stuck in the sand and he starts sweating with the effort. Not cool.

The third reason why the sands are peaceful is the most curious of all. It may be that being nearly naked on a beach has a levelling effect but there is still what the sociologists call social differentiation on the beach, that is class. At the back of the sands are lines of what are often called chalets or huts but here called tents (because they used to be made of canvas). Unlike those of some other beaches, these are taken up in the winter because of the tides. Some are owned by the Council and some are private. Tent occupants are the aristocracy of the sands. Whether by legal or moral right they act as if the piece of beach in front of their tent is theirs. And the tentless hordes act in this way too. The tented are usually residents or the dispersed but visiting families of residents. So life just in front of the tents is rather different from that lower down the beach among the visitors. But even the visitors use their chairs and wind-breaks to establish temporarily private territory and this is respected by others. Further different parts of the beach attract different types of people. For instance, as any beach-goer knows, the area nearest the foot of the steps attracts the most vulgar people: they can't be bothered to walk any further. Old-hands know where the wind blows least. They also know the tides and sit where they will not have to move as the waters come in. Young persons, insofar as there are any, sit near the pub. Old persons sit conveniently near, but not too near the lavatories. What is remarkable is not the differentiation but the mutual deference that goes with it. Sensitivity to space and to time were hallmarks of the old Middle England.

There are however ways in which the sands today are different from those of the past. They do not necessarily make it a worse place to be, but they are all signs of decadence. The first is the most significant. In the old days, that is, up to the Sixties, a family would come to the seaside for a one or two-week holiday. They would stay in a guest house. After their eight o'clock breakfast they would be ejected and not expected back until "tea" at about six. So they would come onto the sands and stay there for about nine hours. Bearing in mind what was said above, this meant that the children were orderly, peaceful and amused themselves inventively or at least contentedly for nine hours. Occasionally, when they showed signs of fractiousness or boredom, the parents would intervene. One way or another, the family behaved sociably for nine hours.

It is rare now for a family to stay all day. Most stay about three hours. Watch a prime site of sand and you will see it occupied by three different families in a day. Even during the three hours, countless expeditions back into the town are mounted in the attempt to stave off boredom, tears or riot. These are accompanied by bribes, money to buy chips, plastic toys, fizzy drinks, more money to spend in the amusement arcade or to go to the funfair.

In short these children have what is sometimes called a low attention span. It should not be called that. That makes it sound like some minor inherited defect. In truth, the children have been extremely badly brought up, over-indulged and taught neither self-control nor the orderly use of time. The seriousness can be seen on the rare occasions when the endless demands of the children for entertainment are thwarted: children as old as 12 go into tears and tantrums. It used to be the pride of Middle England that its children were well-brought up and a crucial part of this was the appropriate use of time, self-control over a long period, and the ability to defer gratification, to wait. Indeed inability to defer gratification is a chief cause of crime: the young offender differs from the non-offender not in wanting something more or different, but in wanting it, in demanding it, in taking it now.

The second sign of decline is related. The modern parent's response to the demands of the children they have failed to socialise is to give in and buy them off, literally with money. The sands used to cost nothing apart from one watery lollipop. Now during the three hour beach session, Mum is continually reaching for her purse and Dad unrolling another fiver. The bribery, of course, does not work. It makes the existing problem worse and introduces another which is the equation of pleasure with expenditure.

And this is related to the last sign of decadence: the use of goods to show off, the acquisition of status not by conduct but by possession. The bleached safety fascists use flags to divide the bay into a swimming and boating area. Every now and then the owners of sailing boats bring them to the shore, launch and set off for a race. In the fifties, these sailors wore saggy blue woollen swimming trunks or costumes and white V-necked cricket type pullovers. Now they wear rubber pixie shoes, rubber trousers and tops, little gloves and life belts. Their boats are similarly over equipped and funded. What has happened to sailing is simply what has happened to golf, running, cricket or any of the games and sports, the corruption of amateurism and the virtues that went with it and their replacement by conspicuous consumption and showing off. Now, it may be that amateurism was, in origin, more an aristocratic than a middle-class virtue, but there is no doubt it became a middle- class virtue through public and grammar school sport, and that if there was one thing the old middle class abhorred it was showing off.

At first sight, the behaviour of Middle England on today's beach is somewhat more reassuring than that seen in some of the other places discussed in this book. Unfortunately a closer look shows the rot has begun to set in even here.

CHAPTER SEVEN

At the airport and abroad

At the airport there is a lady in the café near the departure lounge drinking a cup of coffee. I am looking at her rear. She has spiky hair with red and green streaks. She wears a "top" that is too small for her. As she slumps forward to slurp her coffee, she exposes two or three inches of flesh which cascade down at each side over her trousers, which are also too small for her. In the middle of this roll of floppy pink flesh there is a tattoo with some rude words. When I go round to have a look at her front, I see she has a large ring through her nose. Leave aside, for a moment, the repulsiveness of her get-up, two things are of interest. First, she is in her fifties and the uniform she is in is a youth uniform. The old ME had a key dress rule which was never to look like "mutton dressed as lamb". You age sheep by their teeth. This lady is well over "sixtooth". She should be using dress and make-up to conceal her lumpiness not to parade it. In another phrase of the old ME, we should "act our age". The fads of the young are often tiresome and ugly. But far worse than any sartorial absurdities young people themselves may exhibit are those which occur when middle-aged and elderly people act as if they were young. And this applies to much more than dress. There is something pathetic about oldies using the argot of the young, drinking the drinks the young drink, out of bottles like the young, pretending to know about and like the latest awful tune that is popular with the young. In the culture of ME the duty of the grown ups was to be grown up and to set an example to the young.

However, they also have another obligation. It is a commonplace that sex looms very important for the adolescent and the young married person. An obvious corollary is that sex is not important in understanding or expecting certain standards of children. (This is one reason why Freud who tried to sexualize children, may be at least as important an enemy of ME as Marx.) A less obvious corollary is that sex should become less important as adults age. That is what ME believed. Fifty year olds may retain some interest in sex but they have other more important things to think about. Their appearance should be based on these other important things too. Their suit should show off their membership of the business community. Their looks in general should show judgement, seriousness and dignity not raunchy availability. The sheep-lady at the airport trying to look like lamb is not only breaking an age rule, she is breaking a sex rule. That explains why the sight of her doing so is particularly unattractive. ME, both elderly men and women used to be rather good at cultivating a dress and hair style which played down or ignored sex. They have lost this art, or surrendered it and the result is neither convincing (sexually) or impressive.

The fat lady in the tight clothes with the tattoo and ring is off to Spain or Greece for a holiday. She herself is English so she will be an Englishwoman abroad and be seen by the Spanish and the Greeks as such. The old ME would have said she had an obligation to show off her country in the best light, not to let it down. Not only does she look repulsive and stupidly inappropriate for her age but she makes, in some small way, English women of her age in general look repulsive and silly. The old ME was obsessed by reputation and its understanding of reputation was collective. Its members belonged to a family, a village or street, a school, a firm and a country, and when they behaved badly they damaged not only their own reputation but that of the family etc. When this let-down was of a more serious nature, for instance bearing a child born out of wedlock, the shame at loss of reputation was attached to and felt by far more people than the person who had let others down. Moreover, Middle England knew that reputation is tied up with appearance: what else, for much of the time, can we judge by if not by appearance? Put these two understandings together and you get the rule that one should dress so as not to let down the family, place, class etc to which one belongs.

The tattooed lady is not a rarity. Age distinctions in dress are under constant erosion. What is more serious is the erosion of the idea of group reputation. Not only does that show a lack of consideration for our family, class, countrymen, it shows a diminished sense of community. At the time of writing the media have been full of the exploits of British young people on a Greek island. The men have been exposing their bottoms on the street and the women their chests in bars. Both have been drinking, vomiting and copulating in public. Once again these young people are not that young. "Youth" used to mean teenagers and there are, thank heaven, only seven teen years. But the tawdriness and vulgarity of youth culture now extends down to eight year-olds and up and beyond thirty year-olds. Once again, this youth culture is no respecter of class: in fact, youth is now a class. The bottoms, breasts and vomit exposed without solicitation to all and any are those, amongst others, of Middle England. The media have thoroughly enjoyed the whole episode as have, presumably their readers including their ME readers. While the tone has been a mixture of prurience and mild disapproval, there has been no sense of shame, that these are "our" people and that their behaviour reflects badly on us.

The old ME insistence on a time and place for everything is especially important when apparent deviance occurs. Even in the dull and conformist 1930s and 1950s young people were difficult and deviant but they knew when and where to do it. Recently I went through UK border controls whilst returning to England from France in my car. As I was passing a shed which looked like a down-market car wash, a young man who looked like a down-market car wash attendant stepped out. He wore some sort of scruffy denims and was unshaven. He spoke with an aggressive tone and lower class accent: "Ah long 'ave you bin aht of the UK?" was the gist of the question. He was a member of Her Majesty's Customs and Excise which should, to be kind to them, count as some sort of profession or service. Yet he, like all those scruffy Council school teachers who are seen every year at the annual conferences had no idea how to dress or shave or speak at professional work. The tendency of the professions to talk and look like yobs is now accepted, indeed expected. On my return I saw a catalogue advertising church furnishings and other ecclesiastical supplies. One page displayed models in clerical shirts showing what the self-respecting priest of today should look like. Five out of the six models pictured were unshaven.

The obsession ME had with appearance, like that with accent, requires elaboration. Appearance was a guide to character. Someone who would break the codes of his class on dress or accent might do so where sexual political or business matters were concerned. And rebellious ME youngsters surely shared the same view: when they did dress unconventionally, it was precisely in order to suggest to the world that they had unconventional sexual habits or political commitments. The parents knew that this was sometimes no more than a front, that most

young people who wore corduroys and suede boots or, in the case of girls, duffle coats and jeans, were not wildly promiscuous or about to defect to the Soviet Union. But, in this case, they had another cause for complaint. In this case their offspring were "Exhibitionists". And, of course, they were exhibitionists. They were seeking to make an impression, to stand out and draw attention to themselves. This, though understandable in the young, is according to traditional ethics not a virtue. It is self-centredness, pride and it may also involve an implied sneer at those conventional parents, Middle England itself, from whom the exhibitionists are trying to distance themselves. The actual clothes or accents may be morally trivial: the motives for exhibiting them may be highly morally significant. Moreover exhibitionism involves the MEs in a conspicuousness which is morally dangerous and also a repudiation of one's membership of a social class, that of Middle England.

The old ME saw itself surrounded by several other types of people who were, at the least, "not like us". Some were dangerous in the sense that they were hostile and the rule was that one tried to ignore them lest they be incited to physical hostility. Others were dangerous in that they constituted temptations to which the weaker and stupider members of Middle England might succumb. Common people were bad; far worse was it if you yourself or your children looked common. There was nothing general or vague about being common. Avoiding looking common involved fastidious attention to detail. It was not unknown, for instance, for quite low income respectable families to send their children for elocution lessons or deportment or dancing classes to eradicate the bad habits they had picked up through proximity to common children either via state Council housing or state Council schools. Here's Patrick

Hamilton's 1930's Jenny in *Twenty Thousand Streets under the Sky* (Vintage, 1988).

"There was a great difference between being 'made up' and being 'dolled up,' and it was possible to be made up in a 'common' way. Jenny tolerated nothing even savouring of the 'common' ". Jenny's friend Violet was common and, as was the way, leads Jenny into trouble. Sometimes Violet is worse than common, she is "glaring". "Violet was in a black lustre coat: she wore cheap, gaudy silk stockings of a reddish-brown colour…and a skirt up to her knees. Her face … resembled rich confectionary … Subtlety, or a delicate sense of approach, were means unknown to Violet". Violet talks about common things in a common way. She also has common morals. Jenny wants to go to Lyons. "What's the sense of going to Lyons," said Violet, "if you can get taken?"

Apparent trivia – this, not that type of shoe, saying things this way, waiting this time not that before agreeing to do this or that – were mixed up with more obviously important matters, about sex before marriage or crime in what it was to be common. Precisely because Jenny does not pay enough attention to the warning signs of Violet's common skirt and stockings, she herself winds up involved in sex and crime – a manslaughter. She ends as a prostitute. Looking and being "tarty" were closely linked. For men the equivalent types to the tart or common woman were the rough and the Smart Alec. Once again the minutiae of etiquette and big morals were densely entwined. When the codes about the minutiae were challenged so were the big morals. When Middle England surrendered on gaudy stocking and dropped Aitches, it surrendered on the sanctity of marriage.

CHAPTER EIGHT

At table

You do not ever forget the taste of a toothpaste lollipop. They were part of something then called a "midnight feast". Boys of nine or so at preparatory schools in the 1950s were short of ingredients for feasts of any kind. Eating in the dining hall was closely supervised and stealing spare food difficult. Private caches of things like sweets were forbidden. Thus toothpaste lollipops. Immediately after lights out, take one school issue tin beaker, add water and a squeeze of toothpaste, stir with a toothbrush, leave the toothbrush in the mixture head upwards, place the beaker on the outside of the dormitory window and leave till midnight. Then bash the tin against a pipe to loosen the contents and suck, using the brush as a stick.

Two refinements: some inmates of some boarding schools may question this account on the grounds that a proper prep school of the period would never have permitted the luxury of toothpaste. It is true that few personal luxuries were allowed. Ink, for example was a school monopoly and much watered. But, by the fifties the luxuriant beams of progress and decadence were beginning to penetrate even prep schools and boys were allowed toothpaste. Not all bothered to have it and many did not use it – at least for its usual purpose, hence the feast, but many had it. The alternative was to use nothing or salt. A few boys did use salt.

The reason for placing the beaker outside the window was nothing to do with temperature. The window was compulsorily fully open winter and summer and it was as cold in the dorm as outside. It was that there might be a surprise dorm inspection and the lollipop-making be uncovered and its perpetrators beaten. For the lollipop making and the midnight feast were strictly forbidden. They were forbidden for the same reason that it was forbidden to eat in the classroom, the corridor, or the grounds; for the reason that both school and parents forbade eating in the street. Middle England ate in the dining room and only there. It ate at table not standing up, lying down in dormitories or walking in the street. And it ate together as a school or family, starting together, changing courses together, finishing together and leaving together. This eating together at table and only at table is the key to the old ME culture of food. It was not necessarily proposed as a positive eating culture – "We eat only at table"; more often it can be seen by the behaviour which was loudly and firmly forbidden. "We" must not be late for lunch or dinner. "No, we can't get down before the meal is finished". For day boy and girl pupils, eating on the way to and from school or on the bus is strictly forbidden.

In the culture of Middle England there was "a place and time for everything" and the time for eating was meal-times and the place was, usually, the table. Other parts of the culture flow from it. For instance washing hands before eating or sitting up straight and not putting elbows on the table were enforceable because children were under adult supervision at table. How could any such manners be inculcated and enforced if children ate on their own, in their bedrooms or on the street? The same applies to other aspects of the culture. You opened your mouth to eat, of course, but you did not leave it open. You might speak but not with your mouth full. You would not have much time to speak anyway since, if the house was persuaded by such moral-medical tracts as Lieutenant J P Muller's *My*

System: 15 Minutes Exercise a Day for Health's Sake, the mouth would be otherwise occupied chewing each mouthful thirty times. Knives and forks were placed and held correctly. This, like several of the rules was useful for distinguishing Middle Englanders' eating practices from those of the lower orders who either grasped their irons rudely stabbing and shovelling with the thumb well down the stem or affectedly used them over preciously as if the knife were a pen. ME lowered its cutlery; Lower England kept it aloft, waved it, and even pointed with it.

People spoke quietly at table and not about controversial matters. At tables outside the home ie in public they did not mention private matters. Eaters drank – mostly water – from glasses raising the glass to the mouth and not lowering the mouth to the glass. Everyone served himself in modest portions; no "piling the plate". Salt was poured, again in moderation and mustard put on the side of the plate not liberally shaken or dolloped over the food itself as the lower classes did. Food was not pushed about on the plate. Some rules applied to the food itself. All food was to be eaten, nothing left. Leaving things was a great sin. Whoever was supervising the table "wanted to see a nice clean plate." This was both a matter of not wasting the good things which Father's hard work or Providence had bestowed and also of not insulting other poorer people, often in the Colonies, who would have been grateful for the food so churlishly wasted. Children who suggested that they did not like fat or bread crust or greens or eggs or kippers or whole classes of food such as meat were told not to be cranks. "Fads" were not allowed. They were condemned as a form of irrational self-indulgence and even exhibitionism.

Much of the table training was part of the more general training of children to be obedient, orderly, to respect judgements that society had made about the fitness of foods and to avoid self-centredness and whim and fussiness. The table paid a crucial role in socializing children. The food itself was hedged about with rules. There were usually two courses at lunch or dinner, meat, fish or eggs first then sweet pudding. The meat came with two or more vegetables one of which was always potatoes. Fish sometimes came with only one vegetable and rarely green vegetables apart from peas. Meals were at fixed times. Some households had fixed weekly menus: roast Sunday, cold Monday, mince Wednesday, chops Thursday, fish Friday, sausages Saturday.

Middle England ate out in restaurants rarely especially outside London and the big cities. Eating out was a treat or occasion, a celebration of a birthday or anniversary or because one was away from home on holiday in a hotel. In fact hotel dining rooms were the standard eating-out experience for much of Middle England. Middle England might eat out in hotel or restaurant rarely but the lower classes ate there hardly ever. So the culture in hotels and restaurants was that of Middle England. The rules of the home, the correct behaviour at table, were simply transferred to the restaurant. There might be a small indulgence, a sherry first, a bottle of wine, a Dover sole, some roast duck, a trifle, even a first course, perhaps a mixed hors d'oeuvres with tinned sardines, baby silverskin pickled onions, hard boiled eggs and Danish salami. But The King's Arms or Clark's restaurant was ME cultural territory just as the transport café was working class cultural territory. And to an extent the classes not only ate differently but ate different things when out. Certainly they drank different things. The lower classes did not drink sherry, gin and orange or tonic, Scotch and soda, wine (at least of the French sort) or, in the fifties, much

coffee. Crucially, when children and young people ate out, they did so at table under the supervision of parents and other adults so the general ME culture of eating and good behaviour was enforced.

If you were to try and think of one change, just one, which would blow this culture of eating and of child training to pieces it would not be one concerning any aspect of manners such as the way salt was sprinkled or food not wasted. It would be the condition that made all these aspects possible, eating together at table. The table itself is not, of course, the magic ingredient. What is important is that eating be done under adult control and supervision according to a code of manners with a form, everyone conforming to that form together. The old Middle England did eat away from tables. It ate picnics on rugs and had elevenses off shelves and desks. But even these were governed by collectively sanctioned forms. At cinemas, for instance, eating was confined to an intermission when a girl appeared with a tray of ice-creams. An orderly queue formed, ice-creams were purchased and eaten, and then the films resumed. Today drinks are slurped and sweets eaten throughout. What's eaten, predominately, is pop corn and that results in a stench which pervades the auditorium. Making smells in public used to be thought even worse than shouting. And both were associated with foreigners.

So what has happened to ME eating habits? Children and young people increasingly eat on their own or at any rate away from adult supervision. Old fashioned souls may object to the way young people and not so young people, including those from middle-class provincial homes eat today; the way they slump at table, lean and fork out bits of their friends' food to try, dribble, guffaw and speak loudly of matters which should be private to each other (at a respectable restaurant I recently heard a horribly detailed account of one lady's visit to and participation in a lap-dancing club. She was telling the story three tables away). And all manner of private details are bellowed down mobile phones. In more expensive restaurants it's not lap dancers you hear about but private business. Businessmen treat the restaurant as they do the train, as a private office, they do their deals, rebuke their staff and give orders. This is offensive not only to the other passengers but to the staff to whom they are talking. I recently heard one businessman give his welcoming interview to a new staff member over the phone. We were all treated to the details of his challenges, how he should soon be "embedded in the team", various warnings, reflections on his character, its "positive" features and ones "which need watching where we must build if the relationship is to grow." A column in *The Times* (16.9.2003) reports someone often overhearing, that is being compelled to overhear, confidential business conversations indeed conversations containing information which is price sensitive to stocks. This is not only rude and embarrassing; it is a total confusion of public and private spheres, a distinction that Middle England held most dear – once upon a time. A long time ago.

Then there's the way the new Middle England over-order or over-serve themselves and leave lots of food; the way they eat inappropriate combinations or foods and refuse all manner of good things. They take food at any time and in any order on impulse. When they abandon half-eaten burgers and bags of chips that is, again, on impulse. They drink straight from bottles and cans, and reveal the contents of their unfinished mouthfuls as they speak. But these only happen because the ME family has abandoned its first rule of eating and let its young eat away from the supervised table. People now eat on their own standing up, in trains, malls, buses, streets, offices, classrooms and occasionally in churches. Many of the young eat on their own or with their own age group. That, in terms of the old ME world is total revolution.

It is not a revolution that has been forced on the families of Middle England. McDonald's and the junk food culture have not been forced on an unwilling populace. For some reason the parents have given up their old responsibilities in bringing up their children within an orderly, adult-dominated home and surrendered their faith in their own culture. The result is music to their old enemies, the lefties' ears: the supposedly ME young when they eat are now indistinguishable from the lower orders. Unfortunately the consequences go far beyond the table. What has been surrendered is not table etiquette but a concern for and a distinct way of bringing up children. If this were the working class we were talking about, the term used to describe those who have so abjectly surrendered would be class traitors.

CHAPTER NINE

In court

In the Magistrates' Court, those charged and waiting to appear are sitting at the back with me. I am the only person at the back who is not wearing trainers and either jeans or tracksuits. Defendants do not dress formally anymore to go to court. They wear the same clothes they go assaulting or burglaring in or indeed would wear for a day out shopping. Presumably their defence solicitor has not advised them to dress respectfully because he doesn't think it would make any difference. Perhaps he is right. Perhaps it would not make any difference with today's magistrates. It used to, when the court was Middle England territory. The defendants are charged with being drunk, harassing their "partners", Actual Bodily Harm, resisting arrest, driving while disqualified, stealing men's toiletries from department stores (to pay their drug dealers for drugs), failing to stop and report an accident, stealing a couple of thousand pounds' worth of clothes, threatening to kill people, stealing cars and burning them, and possessing drugs. Actually, although some are charged with having drugs, drugs can get them out of as well as into trouble. One defence is that the defendant is not normally like this ie attacking policemen or burning cars; he was under the influence of drugs! Often there are several offences or the accused is already on bail, or has broken bail terms.

They are young, mostly male and from the lower orders. This last condition emerges when they are asked how much they can afford to pay if or when they are fined. Those who are working seem to earn about £12,000 but some of this is going on paying or more usually not paying fines. Several have not made payments. This raises an interesting puzzle: if they are paying past fines then they cannot be expected to afford to pay a new fine. If they aren't paying, will they pay if a fine is imposed?

Just as several have failed to pay fines, others have disobeyed various court orders such as not going near the people they are charged with harassing. Some have disobeyed and not turned up at all. Sometimes evidence such as CCTV footage has not turned up or there hasn't been time for various reports, or a defendant wants to change his solicitor and the new solicitor is not there. So what the court does most of the time is ask whether procedures have been complied with, find they haven't and adjourn the case after appropriate arguments about whether to remand in custody or on bail whether the charged will respect bail, whether he has an address, whether he might offend in the bail period and so on. In a sense what the court does is talk about itself and its own procedures and whether the person charged will comply with them.

Put it another way, what is not talked about is what those charged are alleged to have done. Usually they plead guilty anyway so all the interest is on the sentence and mitigating and administrative matters. The actual offence is briefly described by the prosecution: "he fell over in the road drunk" or "he hit two men in a pub" or "His car hit another on a roundabout and the person in the other car hurt her back and neck". After the guilty plea – which has been made as early as possible to win as many points as possible by cooperating with the police and with the procedures, the defence solicitor spends most of his time explaining mitigating circumstances. Thus he got drunk because he was depressed and he was depressed because he lost his job, his mother or his partner left him.

Sometimes he gets drunk because he is depressed. In other cases he gets depressed because he drinks too much. He fails to report the accident on the roundabout because he is in a hurry to get his work done. Sometimes the mitigating circumstances are to do with procedure. He pleaded guilty at the very first opportunity as mentioned above or in one case he turned himself in. Or he has found new lodging further away from the partner he harassed so it will be safe to remand him on bail. In one hilarious case the defendant offered as evidence of total cooperation that he had been so drunk when he fell over in the road in front of the police car that he couldn't remember and was therefore content to trust the police's version of events. For this act of trust, the defending solicitor thought he might have his fine reduced.

Most of the solicitors are young and lounge about in the awkward way young people have. Received Pronunciation is rare. Some speak so badly that I could not make out what they were saying. They use phrases such as "to facilitate the procedure at this moment in time" and describe offences as "one-off". One of the male solicitors has a bracelet and two have beards. What the Middle-England magistrates are confronted with then, as they gaze down from their bench, is a view of everything the old Middle England loathed, the lower orders at their worst and the middle classes failing their own class. The three magistrates themselves look very middle class and sound it. They are reassuring old and conservatively dressed too. They are unfailingly polite and the business of the court is carried out with exemplary middle-class efficiency. But appearances and sounds are deceptive. The question is not whether the magistrates look the part. It is whether Middle-English values dominate the court. They do not.

Two sorts of values dominate the court. There are the values of the defence which are a hotchpotch of the usual liberal excuses. Apart from the poor lad being under the influence of drugs and thus not himself, he is "susceptible to the influence of others". He is easily led, got into the wrong company. This is a wonderfully agile excuse. Thus in addition to blaming others it can turn out that the accused has now come under "good influences", perhaps a new girl friend, so to put him inside would be to deprive him of these good influences. And again, to put a person so susceptible to influence inside would make him influenced by the bad people in prison, There's the usual babble about him needing his esteem boosting or the offence being a "cry for help". One old excuse, that the accused has mental problems has been dusted down and re-modelled for the new procedurally obsessed age. What counts now is not being depressed or paranoid but offering and indeed wishing to see a psychiatrist, actually showing an appointment card and having made an appointment with a drugs rehabilitation unit. Then there are the usual staples such as dyslexia, child abuse and any form of illness. Occasionally the reasoning is fantasy-like. One solicitor pointed out that his client, who had been in and out of prison, with lots of previous convictions, was the sort of chap who couldn't go five days without committing an offence. Or rather he used to be that sort of chap. In the last three months he had totally changed and done nothing wrong at all except one case of driving disqualified and hitting a policeman, so he should not be sent to prison this time.

It's difficult to say whether anyone, the magistrates, the defendants or the solicitors believe this nonsense. But everyone seems to go along with it. The excuses about depression and the rest are not uttered or

received with much conviction. Conviction is almost totally lacking, especially conviction about the offence. And so is any sense of offence being taken, of the magistrates being offended or morally indignant.

Once upon a time in the 1960s, two teenage cults, Mods and Rockers, rioted on Margate front. They fought each other. When they came to court they were addressed by the Chairman of the Bench, a certain Dr George Simpson. He denounced them as "petty, sawdust Caesars". The whole affair caused a great stir in the press. A sociologist, Dr Stanley Cohen wrote a book in which the incident was discussed. The stir, he called a moral panic. The rioters he called folk devils. From about that time a way of looking at the justice system emerged. It argued that the court, as well as imposing the law was imposing middle-class, middle-aged and often ignorant standards. Sometimes this view stressed the idea that if we can understand the context in which apparently deviant acts take place then we can understand and sympathize with those who do them. Sometimes it argues that the courts – and indeed the schools and social services – are middle- class institutions which apply laws not impersonally but with certain class feelings of decency, respectability and outrage at their flouting.

The mild version of this theme has some truth to it. George Simpson did not just apply the law, he added a commentary which resonated with the feelings of many ME families. And why not? It is good that law should reflect a general morality. He did not break or bend the law. He explained why it had to be applied. This view, that courts stood not just for the law but for ideas such as decency was widespread. It meant that when someone offended particular laws the court not only applied the law impersonally but expressed moral outrage. That moral outrage was, as often as not, outrage at offences against the morality of Middle England.

This expression of outrage or moral condemnation was almost totally missing from the court I attended. As I say, there was little time spent on the actual offence. Procedure was what dominated. It was the second dominant value system, even more important than the liberal excuse culture. Although most of the offences were not the gravest, most of the offenders had records with lots of offences, records of not paying fines, not obeying court orders. These can be translated from procedural to moral terms. In moral terms these can be cast as not being truly sorry or resolved to mend their ways, being obdurate. So even the procedure could have been moralized. It wasn't. The courts like the schools used to be bastions of Middle England, places where its values were declared and transmitted. They are not any more. Some of the magistrates have themselves embraced amoral proceduralism, others are no doubt prevented from voicing the values of their class by their respect for the new procedures. They have been outmanoeuvred by the law and procedure makers. Either way, Middle England has lost a crucial power base.

These observations are made about magistrates' courts. One question sometimes asked about higher, jury courts is why Middle Englanders who used to be so meticulous about discharging their public duties, are now so reluctant to do jury service. The answer would seem to be that these higher courts, like the magistrates' courts are no longer places where Middle England feels at home. What is true of the courts may also be true of the state school and the NHS surgery. In all these Middle England is being squeezed out by the forces of intellectual liberalism and state proceduralism.

CHAPTER TEN

Conclusion: a future for Middle England?

The main purpose of this study was not to decide whether the various changes that Middle England has undergone are for the better or for the worse. It was to show that the old Middle England has changed so much that it has really ceased to exist. It has surrendered those values and that behaviour which were central to its identity.

In the shopping mall and at the airport we found ME trying to look like the lower classes and the middle aged trying to look like youth. The old ME devoted its life to showing as much distance between it and the lower classes as possible. The old ME valued effort, discipline, planning, prudence, economy, seriousness, waiting for gratification and the avoidance of debt. Its successors' values can be seen in the supermarket and shopping mall, and they are the opposite, a preference for easiness, a refusal to wait for satisfaction, a lack of discipline and prudence with money and credit, little planning, instead a reliance on impulse both in shopping and eating, wastefulness, feeling good rather than being good, frivolity, not making children contribute to family chores.

The failure to control children in public, or to ask them to do anything helpful were seen at the swimming pool too. On the beach the adults pandered to the children's reduced attention span and indulged them. The old ME prided itself on its control of children in public. And the new ME adults themselves behaved in these places in ways their grandparents would have abhorred; speaking badly, shouting, eating anywhere and anyhow, showing off with their clothes and manners, being familiar with comparative strangers, conspicuously consuming things.

These were habits the old Middle England associated with oiks, spivs, tarts and yobs. Now it behaves like them. In other places it is not so much or not only that it behaves like them. It is more that it has ceded ground to them. Increasingly Middle England has deserted the pub. In the court it is still there but it no longer dares speak its strong moral views. It has given in to bureaucratic proceduralism and liberalism. It has largely retreated from the church too or accepted there other forms of liberalism, vulgarity and childishness it once would have excoriated. The old Middle England, its values attitudes and behaviour are now rarely seen in public. Maybe they are still there in home, in secret, but in public life Middle England has surrendered.

Is this the end of the story? Not quite. There's one more brief visit to be paid, and it's to a place which might give a glimpse of the future Middle England. The university contains the next generation. It also contains, if we are to believe endless complaints from socialists in and outside the government too many middle-class students. It is, allegedly an institution whose values and admission criteria favour the middle class. So what are they like these "middle-class students"?

Even the most extreme socialist would not claim that all students are middle class. So the more pertinent question is; in what ways do the middle-class students differ from the others? They certainly look the same. It is difficult to tell the daughter of a doctor from the daughter of an unemployed miner, indeed sometimes from the son of an unemployed miner. There is now a student or young person's uniform which over-rides class barriers. It is the

Middle-England-origin students who now dress down to the lower class style. Accents are not so easily changed but ME-origin students make a valiant effort to speak lazily, to mumble, to affect lower-class patterns and to strive for inarticulacy and a loudly professed enthusiasm for football. In fairness and explanation, it must immediately be added that the lecturers and tutors occasionally talk like yobs too – and look like them. One lecturer claims to be the only person in his large department to wear proper shoes. It is not unknown for a lecturer to be unshaven. With the lowering of the age of majority and the lowering of the quality of the lecturers – consolidated by political correctness – any interest in the moral standards and welfare of the student has gone. Gone, that is, from the lecturers. Were one to try to help a student maintain moral standards it would be seen as interference and possibly a cause for sanctions to be imposed – on the lecturer.

One has to remember that university lecturers aspire to be professional people. That used to mean setting an example in their own behaviour. Apart from a tolerated tendency to eccentricity, they were, like schoolmasters and mistresses and lawyers and clergymen part of Middle England. They are not any more. Small wonder that their students are not either. Lecturers tell me of students talking during lectures when they should be silent – just as their parents talk in church.. Outside when they should talk, they shout. They eat and drink during lectures; indeed they eat and drink anywhere but at table during mealtimes. One matter that seems to vary among universities is lateness. Lecturers from some universities complain of students being late for lectures, coming not in a block five minutes late but a dribble during the first 15 and making a comprehensible start impossible. Yet even as late as the 1970s in some Oxford lectures one could be turned away for being more than two minutes late. Others complain of students entering lecturers' rooms either without knocking or without waiting to be invited after knocking. They fail to use lecturers' titles or say please and thank you. They fail to apologize for this rudeness or their lateness. And the lateness extends beyond lectures. They are late with their projects, late for tutorials, late for everything. This is encouraged by some universities which are enthusiastic in finding "exceptional circumstances" to excuse it. Several times in this short book we have noticed how a concern for time, doing things on time and at the right time used to be a chief defining characteristic of Middle England.

Yet other lecturers report that students have difficulty writing neatly and legibly. This is partly because they seldom have to. Their supervisors allow typescript and for PC reasons (getting rid of cultural variables) have often substituted forms for essays. Even the students' lack of use of lecturers' titles merely follows the lecturers' own reference to each other in casual and personal terms. And, in several universities, those same lecturers have gone along with an egalitarian reform to list them along with the secretaries and other employees as "staff". Why should they attract respect from others when they don't have it for themselves? The respect should not just be for their high qualification and wisdom. It should be because they are adults. What the lecturers are disavowing is not just their professional status but their role as adults. Old ME thought that adulthood carried with it specific and unconditional responsibilities. And the student side of this is the abdication of any sense of deference to greater age. They are not the only ones. It is a general phenomenon that society does not value its older, wiser members. The loss of adult responsibility and deference to age and the lateness and rudeness and bad example of the lecturers are more significant than the more usually cited drug-taking and promiscuity at university. Because of them, both on the part of students and even more of "staff", the university has simply ceased to be part of Middle England.

Occasionally a rare academic will break rank and bemoan the academic standards of today's students. Our concern is not with their academic but their social and moral standards. More particularly, we cannot see anything in students' behaviour which suggests they will prove to be the trusty guardians of the virtues and attitudes of the old Middle England in the future.

It is sometimes said that these virtues and attitudes were born out of necessity, out of war or what would now be regarded as comparative poverty. Neither are adequate explanations: there are plenty of poor and war-stricken people who have not evolved the values of the old Middle England. Perhaps a war, a long and horrific one or an economic collapse of similar proportions might provide the impetus for a return to these values, but I doubt it. I see nothing in the public behaviour of the old, the middle-aged or the young which suggests that the old Middle England will survive or return. What the precise bill for the oik victory will be and who will pay it, we shall have to wait to see.

Biographical Note

Dr Digby Anderson has been associated with The Social Affairs Unit for twenty four years. He was its founder Director in 1980. His books as author or contributing editor for the Unit include **The War on Wisdom** (2003), **Losing Friends** (2002) and **Faking It: The Sentimentalisation of Modern Society** (1998). He has been a columnist for *The Times, The Sunday Times, The Sunday Telegraph, The Spectator* and in the USA for *National Review.*